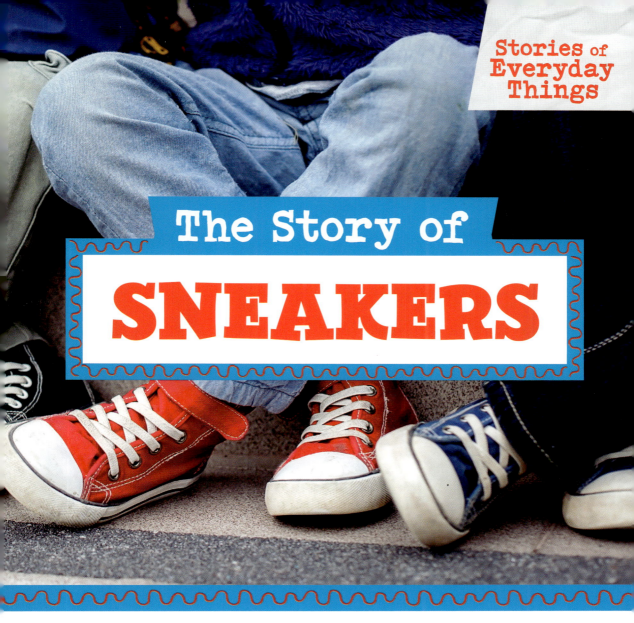

Stories of Everyday Things

The Story of
SNEAKERS

by Mae Respicio

PEBBLE
a capstone imprint

Published by Pebble, an imprint of Capstone
1710 Roe Crest Drive, North Mankato, Minnesota 56003
capstonepub.com

Copyright © 2025 by Capstone. All rights reserved. No part of this publication may be reproduced in whole or in part, or stored in a retrieval system, or transmitted in any form or by any means, electronic, mechanical, photocopying, recording, or otherwise, without written permission of the publisher.

Library of Congress Cataloging-in-Publication Data is available on the Library of Congress website.
ISBN: 9780756582029 (hardcover)
ISBN: 9780756582159 (paperback)
ISBN: 9780756582081 (ebook PDF)

Summary: Trainers. Runners. Kicks. No matter what you call your them, sneakers are a great way to show off your style. But who invented this famous footwear? How are sneakers made? And how do they end up in stores and closets around the world? Find out in this informational book all about sneakers.

Editorial Credits
Editor: Alison Deering; Designer: Jaime Willems; Media Researcher: Jo Miller; Production Specialist: Whitney Schaefer

Image Credits
Alamy: Pictures Now, 10; Getty Images: Hulton Archive, 7, kvkirillov, 8; Shutterstock: 2p2play, 11, 8th.creator, 26, cunaplus, 19, dreamnikon, 20, EmilioZehn, 15, i viewfinder, 21, Itxu, 9, Back Cover, Lithiumphoto, 14, LittleMiss, Cover, Master1305, 5, Myroslava Gerber, 24, panpote, 18, pio3, 22, Roman Samborskyi, 13, ShutterBri, 27, Simikov, 16, Studio Romantic, 17, Tada Images, 25, Tomsickova Tatyana, 1, 23, Yuriy Golub, 29; SuperStock: Science Museum/SSPL/Science and Society, 6

Design Elements: Shutterstock: Luria, Pooretat moonsana

Any additional websites and resources referenced in this book are not maintained, authorized, or sponsored by Capstone. All product and company names are trademarks™ or registered® trademarks of their respective holders.

Printed in the United States   5997

Table of Contents

The World of Sneakers 4

Sneakers Through Time 6

Creating Cool Kicks 14

Getting Sneakers To You 20

Sneakers in the Spotlight 24

Design Your Own Sneakers! 28

Glossary 30

Read More 31

Internet Sites 31

Index 32

About the Author 32

Words in bold appear in the glossary.

The World of Sneakers

Trainers. Runners. Kicks. What's another name for them? Sneakers! Lace them up. Run around. Show off your style!

People all around the world wear sneakers. They are worn on playgrounds and on sports fields. They are even seen on the red carpet! Sneakers are a part of everyday life. But how did they become so popular?

Sneakers Through Time

Sneakers have been around since the 1800s. In 1832, Wait Webster **patented** plimsolls. These shoes were made of cloth. Their soles were made of rubber. They had no right or left foot!

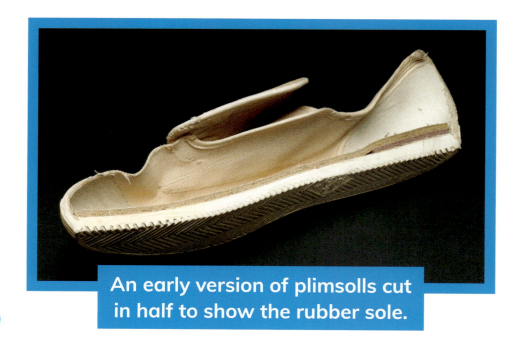

An early version of plimsolls cut in half to show the rubber sole.

Things started changing in 1839. An inventor named Charles Goodyear discovered a new process. It was called **vulcanization**. It turned rubber into a flexible material. This made shoes more comfortable. It was also one step toward inventing the sneaker.

Charles Goodyear

A pair of Keds

In 1916, the United States Rubber Company created another kind of sneaker. They were called Keds. At first, they were named Peds. This came from the Latin word for feet. But another company already had that name. Eventually the name Keds stuck!

Keds were designed for sports. The tops were made from thick **canvas**. The soles were made from sturdy rubber. Rubber soles gave the shoes a much better grip. In 1917, Keds became the first sneakers to be **mass-produced**.

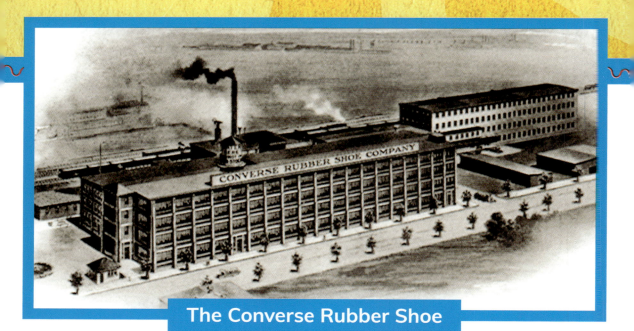

The Converse Rubber Shoe Company factory

The real game changer was Marquis Converse. He worked at the U.S. Rubber Company. But in 1908 he started the Converse Rubber Shoe Company. In 1917, he created the Converse All Star.

Basketball player and salesman Charles "Chuck" Taylor later promoted the shoe. He helped make them famous. These sneakers are some of the most **iconic** in sports history. They are still made today.

Many popular brands also make sports sneakers. Two of the most famous are Nike and Adidas.

Nike and Adidas are some of today's most popular sneaker brands.

In the early 1900s, people wore sneakers mostly for sports. But that changed in the 1950s. People began wearing them for a different reason—fashion.

Actor James Dean was known to wear Converse All Stars. This made sneakers even more popular, especially with young people.

Where does the word sneaker come from? It comes from how quiet the shoes are. That's because of the rubber. Sneakers let you sneak up on people!

Creating Cool Kicks

Today, sneakers are not just for sports. They look cool too! Every sneaker starts with a design. Designers think about style and shape. They also consider comfort. They make models and **mock-ups**.

A designer cuts out a pattern for a pair of shoes.

Next it's on to the factory! Each sneaker needs a **mold.** This is called a shoe last. What shape is it in? A foot! This helps every sneaker fit properly.

shoe molds

Sneakers are made from raw materials. These can include leather and **synthetic** fabrics. Rubber is used for soles.

shoe soles

A factory worker uses machinery to create a new pair of shoes.

It takes people and machines to make sneakers. Laser machines cut the materials. This makes different parts. There is the top part. The bouncy bottom is the outsole. The middle is the midsole. It is a type of cushion. What for? Comfort.

Next, the parts are stitched together. This is often done by hand. The parts move through an **assembly line**. People use machines to put all the pieces together.

Laces come next. They are added to each shoe. Every sneaker is inspected. Is the stitching correct? Is the **logo** in the proper place? Check!

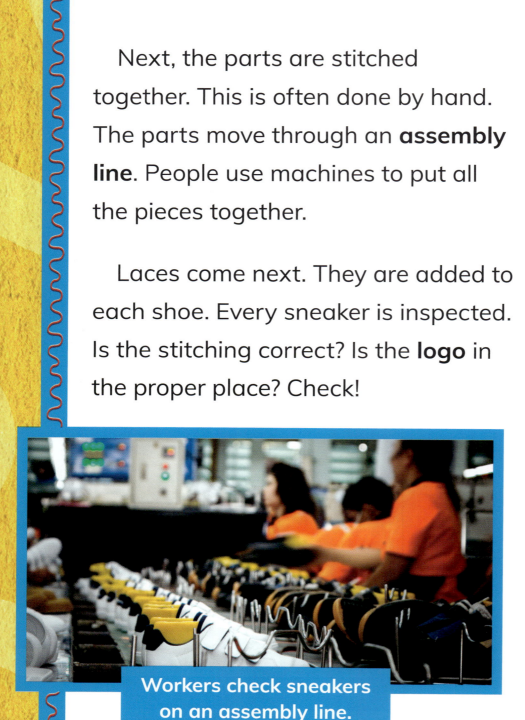

Workers check sneakers on an assembly line.

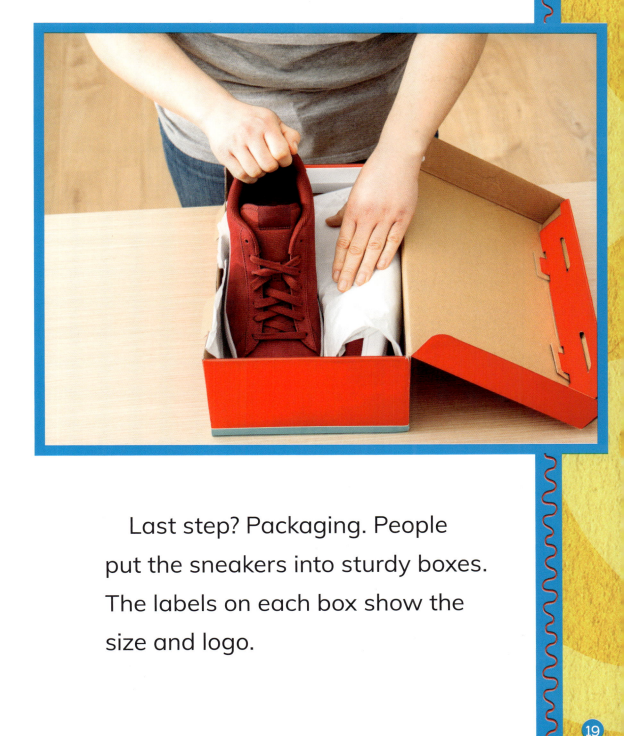

Last step? Packaging. People put the sneakers into sturdy boxes. The labels on each box show the size and logo.

Getting Sneakers To You

How do sneakers get from the factory to you? **Distribution**. Boxes of sneakers are loaded onto trucks. Some are shipped in containers. Some go directly to stores. Most will go to warehouses and distribution centers.

What are distribution centers? It is where sneakers from different factories come together. Why? To sort them. This is done by **conveyor** machines.

Boxes move down a conveyor belt.

Next comes another journey. This time to stores. Once again, the boxes are loaded onto trucks, ships, and planes.

Some sneakers are shipped locally. Others travel far. They go to stores all over the world.

Now are they ready to be worn? Soon! First you must choose your shoes. You can shop online. Or you can visit a store. At last, your sneakers have reached you!

Sneakers in the Spotlight

Today, sneakers are very popular. How many pairs of sneakers does the average American own? Six!

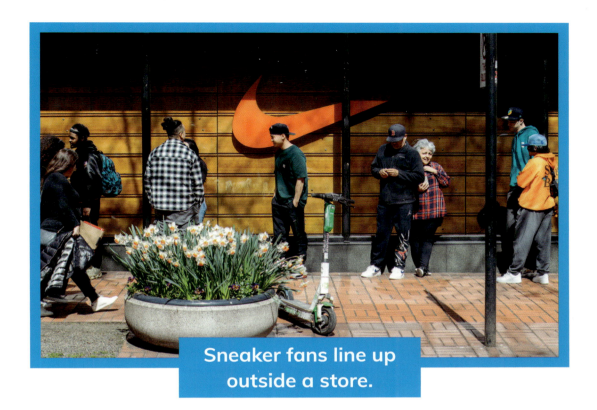

Sneaker fans line up outside a store.

What brand sells the most sneakers around the world? Nike. They sell more than 780 million pairs each year. Wow! Some fans even collect sneakers. They call themselves sneakerheads.

A display of Nike Jordan shoes

Some athletes have sneakers named after them. One famous shoe is the Air Jordan. These sneakers are named after basketball player Michael Jordan. The logo shows him going for a slam dunk!

Whatever you wear them for, one thing is clear. People around the world love and wear sneakers. They are a part of our everyday lives.

Design Your Own Sneakers!

Anyone can design their own sneakers! All it takes is creativity, color, and a blank pair of shoes.

What You Need

- paper
- fabric markers
- a pair of white canvas sneakers

What You Do

1. Brainstorm your design on paper. Express your own style!

2. Use fabric markers to draw your design on your sneakers.

3. Follow the directions on the fabric markers to create your design. Sometimes, you might need to use a hair dryer. Ask an adult for help.

4. Slip on your sneakers. Show off your new kicks!

Glossary

assembly line (uh-SEM-blee LYN)—an arrangement of workers in a factory; work passes from one person to the next person until the job is done.

canvas (KAN-vuhs)—a strong, heavy cloth

conveyor (kuhn-VAY-uhr)—a mechanical device for carrying packages from place to place

distribution (dis-truh-BYOO-shuhn)—the act or process of giving out or delivering something

iconic (ahy-KON-ik)—widely recognized and respected

logo (LOH-goh)—a symbol of a company's brand

mass-produce (mas-pruh-DOOS)—making products in large quantities by using machines and dividing work into simpler tasks to be done by people

mock-up (MOK-uhp)—a full-size example of a proposed design

mold (MOHLD)—a model of an object

patent (PAT-uhnt)—the process of obtaining a legal document to have the right to make or sell a product

synthetic (sin-THET-ik)—something that is made by people rather than found in nature

vulcanization (vuhl-kuhn-ih-ZAY-shuhn)—an industrial process that strengthens natural rubber

Read More

Bell, Samantha S. *You Can Work in Fashion.* North Mankato, MN: Capstone Press, 2019.

Doeden, Matt. *Basketball Shoes, Shorts, and Style.* North Mankato, MN: Capstone Press, 2022.

Sichol, Lowey Bundy. *From an Idea to Nike: How Marketing Made Nike a Global Success.* Boston: Houghton Mifflin Harcourt, 2019.

Internet Sites

Britannica Kids: Shoe
kids.britannica.com/students/article/shoe/277037

Kiddle: Athletic Shoe Facts for Kids
kids.kiddle.co/Athletic_shoe

Time for Kids: Trash to Treasure
timeforkids.com/g34/trash-to-treasure-2/

Index

Adidas, 11
assembly lines, 18
Converse, 10–11, 12
Dean, James, 12
design, 14
distribution, 20, 21, 22
factories, 15, 17, 21
fashion, 12
Goodyear, Charles, 7
Jordan, Michael, 26
Keds, 8–9
logos, 18, 19, 26
materials, 16
molds, 15
Nike, 11, 25, 26
parts, 17, 18
plimsolls, 6
rubber, 6, 7, 9, 13, 16
sneakerheads, 25
sports, 4, 9, 12, 14
Taylor, Charles, 11
United States Rubber Company, 8, 10
vulcanization, 7
Webster, Wait, 6

About the Author

Mae Respicio is a nonfiction writer and middle grade author whose novel, *The House That Lou Built*, won an Asian/Pacific American Libraries Association Honor Award and was an NPR Best Book. Mae lives with her family in California. Some of her favorite everyday things include books, beaches, and ube ice cream.